HOW TO DEAL WITH DIFFICULT PEOPLE

Effective Tips to Deal With Stubborn People

(How to Deal With Nasty Customers and Demanding Bosses)

Yvette Rouse

Published by Sharon Lohan

© **Yvette Rouse**

All Rights Reserved

How to Deal With Difficult People: Effective Tips to Deal With Stubborn People (How to Deal With Nasty Customers and Demanding Bosses)

ISBN 978-1-990334-76-4

All rights reserved. No part of this guide may be reproduced in any form without permission in writing from the publisher except in the case of brief quotations embodied in critical articles or reviews.

Legal & Disclaimer

The information contained in this book is not designed to replace or take the place of any form of medicine or professional medical advice. The information in this book has been provided for educational and entertainment purposes only.

The information contained in this book has been compiled from sources deemed reliable, and it is accurate to the best of the Author's knowledge; however, the Author cannot guarantee its accuracy and validity and cannot be held liable for any errors or omissions. Changes are periodically made to this book. You must consult your doctor or get professional medical advice before using any of the suggested remedies, techniques, or information in this book.

Upon using the information contained in this book, you agree to hold harmless the Author from and against any damages, costs, and expenses, including any legal fees potentially resulting from the application of any of the information provided by this guide. This disclaimer applies to any damages or injury caused by the use and application, whether directly or indirectly, of any advice or information presented, whether for breach of contract, tort, negligence, personal injury, criminal intent, or under any other cause of action.

You agree to accept all risks of using the information presented inside this book. You need to consult a professional medical practitioner in order to ensure you are both able and healthy enough to participate in this program.

Table of Contents

INTRODUCTION 1

CHAPTER 1: TYPES OF DIFFICULT PEOPLE 3

CHAPTER 2: THE PASSIVE-AGGRESSIVE............................ 10

CHAPTER 3: TYPES OF DIFFICULT PEOPLE 22

CHAPTER 4: IDENTIFYING A DIFFICULT PERSON............... 35

CHAPTER 5: EMPATHISE AND NEUTRALISE...................... 44

CHAPTER 6: WHY DEALING WITH STRESS IS IMPORTANT FOR DEALING WITH DIFFICULT PEOPLE 58

CHAPTER 7: ATTITUDE TRANSFER..................................... 63

CHAPTER 8: HOW TO HANDLE GOSSIP AND WORKPLACE BULLIES 70

CHAPTER 9: WHY PEOPLE ARE DIFFICULT 79

CHAPTER 10: FIGHT ONLY THE BATTLES WORTH FIGHTING 93

CHAPTER 11: CHANGE YOUR BEHAVIOR......................... 101

CHAPTER 12: FIND A WAY TO COMMUNICATE OR WORK TOGETHER.. 113

CHAPTER 13: CAN YOU BE FRIENDS WITH YOUR EMPLOYEES? 117

CHAPTER 14: AN INCOMPETENT EMPLOYEE 129

CONCLUSION 146

Introduction

Have you ever tried to move with someone or try to connect but the person seem to be difficult in getting along with?

Or you have a boss at work or a superior in you working place that makes work time uneasy and life difficult for you at times?

Or perhaps you have a friend that all most all of the time there is always communication break or misunderstandings and after you've tried all your best, nothing seems to change?

Trying to get along with a very difficult person can be very tiring and hard especially when it is under a must. But there is always around different problems. If there is a will, there is always a way.

Dealing with a difficult person has been made easy following the steps and method revealed in this book.

The steps and methods divulged in this book are tested and trusted methods that have really helped and worked for the author. And It comprises of gathered experience form other close associates too.

You will learn a deep perspective on how to deal with any difficult person no matter what.

Chapter 1: Types Of Difficult People

In learning how to deal with difficult people, the first thing you have to do is to identify which type of difficult person you are trying to cope with. In reality, there are many different kinds of difficult people. Some are actually a combination of two, three, or four personalities. But for the purpose of this eBook, we will focus on the four main types. The types can obviously be a male or female, but for the sake of consistency, we will refer to the types as a female. Here they are:

The Four Types of Difficult People

Type 1: Bossy (The Manipulator)

The first type is the Bossy person. You can call her "The Manipulator." This type of difficult person is, as the name suggests, officious and a dictator. She always wants what she wants, right here and right now. She has this mentality of "I get what I want." She feels helpless and depressed when things don't go her way or when circumstances are out of her control. You feel like a puppet when you are with her.

Her negative qualities are:

domineering

egotistic

arrogant

impatient

oppressive

On the other hand, she also has positive qualities such as:

confident

competent

revolutionary

competitive

Type 2: Negative (The Pessimist)

The second type is the Negative person. She is also known as "The Pessimist." She always thinks negative of everything and everybody. She is always distrustful of people in general, often doubting their intentions. She thinks ill of others, assumes that others are always thinking negative as well, and expects the worst in all situations. Most of the time, she worries and couldn't see the opportunities in inconveniences. She is very hard to please, complaining is her habit, and dispiriting things spew out of her mouth all the time. You feel like you are carrying a heavy weight on your shoulders when with her.

The negative qualities may be:

cynical

distrustful

hopeless

discouraging

unmotivated

While her positive qualities may be:

cautious

observant

Type 3: Needy (The Leech)

The third type is the Needy person, otherwise called "The Leech." She always needs validation from others, and has very low self-esteem. She thinks that other people are responsible for her happiness that's why she is miserable alone. She doesn't know how to do anything by herself because she wants other people to do everything for her. And to top it all off, she's always fuming and irritated when she feels that she is not being noticed or not attended to. When with her, you feel like she is sucking the life out of you because of her numerous and constant demands.

Her negative qualities may be:

incompetent

insecure

sensitive

quick-tempered

irresponsible

While her positive qualities may be:

passionate

caring

thoughtful

Type 4: Tactless (The Big Mouth)

The fourth type is the Tactless person. She is also called "The Big Mouth." She is super frank and candid that most often she does not think at all every time she speaks. She does not care about the feelings of others and just wants to let go the first thought or idea that comes into her mind. Highly opinionated and blunt, she believes that what she knows is always right. When with her, you are constantly aware that you will be embarrassed at any given time both by what she will say about you and what she will speak about other people as well.

Her negative qualities may be:

apathetic

clueless

sarcastic

narrow-minded

know-it-all

full of negative pride

While her positive qualities may be:

honest

transparent

concerned

The next four chapters will give you essential tips on how to specifically and successfully deal with each of these types of difficult people. Read on!

Chapter 2: The Passive-Aggressive

A passive-aggressive can be defined as a person who appears to conform or act suitably but is actually behaving in a negative manner and is resisting passively. Actions done by passive-aggressive people can be as simple as making excuses for being late or as serious as sabotaging another person's success and well-being.

A person can be considered a chronic passive-aggressive if he has the following characteristics:

• He is very unreasonable to deal with.

• He is unpleasant to be with.

• He seldom expresses his hostility in a direct manner.

• He repeats his deceptive behaviors over time.

A passive-aggressive person can choose to direct his actions towards a group or only to one person. There are a wide range of possible causes for the deep-seated and complex behaviors of passive-aggressive people. But whatever the cause may be, you do not really want to be on the receiving end of their masked hostility. Here are techniques you can use in dealing with passive-aggressive people in different situations:

Do not overreact so you can lessen misunderstandings and personalization

When you are dealing with someone who is possibly a passive-aggressive, avoidjumping to negative conclusions. What you can do is to think of several ways of looking at the situation before you react. For instance, when a colleague doesn't reply to the email that you sent, do not immediately think that he ignores your suggestions because it is possible that he needs more time to digest the suggestions that you have given before he replies to you. When you stop yourself from personalizing the behaviors of other people, you will be able to understand their behaviors in a more objective manner. Always keep in mind that a person does what he does because of"him"more than because of"you". You can prevent misunderstandings by expanding your perspective.

But if you think a colleague has evidently shown behavioral patterns of being passive-aggressive, you can use any of the action steps discussed below:

As much as possible, keep your distance from a passive-aggressive person

There are times when it is really harder to deal with people who are passive aggressive compared to those who are directly hostile. A colleague who is openly aggressive to you will always be direct in his actions and words which will allow you to predict his next moves. In contrast, a passive-aggressive colleague may smile in front of you while secretly sabotaging you. A passive-aggressive colleague works based on a hidden script and you can never too sure when you might be harmed by his evil plans. When you confront a passive-aggressive, it is expected that he will simply deny his involvement. This is the reason why you need to be cautious when dealing with a passive-aggressive.

As much as possible, you should stay away from a passive-aggressive person.

Do not attempt to change a passive-aggressive

Some people attempt to change the negative behaviors of a chronic passive-aggressive by spending a lot of time talking to them. These endeavors are really commendable but you could only end up disappointed and frustrated. The root causes of passive aggressiveness are deep-rooted and very complex. Someone who is passive-aggressive can only change when he eventually achieve self-awareness and becomes more mature. Always remember that it is not really your responsibility to change a passive-aggressive. The most effective method for dealing with a passive-aggressive is to concentrate not on altering his behaviors and attitudes but on firmly taking charge of your own behaviors and attitudes.

Do not allow yourself to be sucked in

When you bear the brunt of the behavior of a passive-aggressive, it is quite understandable for you to feel upset. Your desire to retaliate openly through arguments and sharp language is understandable. You may even think of using passive-aggressive schemes yourself. However, those two approaches are not really helpful. Remember, the passive-aggressive person you are dealing with will only counter your open accusations with denial. He may even claim to be a victim of your hostility. During all these, you will end up frustrated for having allowed this troublemaker to take away your composure. You do not need to give him the power to change you into the kind of person you do not really want to become.

When you are in a fairly mild situation, you can opt to display superior composure by using humor appropriately

If you can, you can use humor as an effective tool for communication. When you are able to use it appropriately, humor can neutralize difficult behaviors while shining light on the truth. When you can use humor appropriately, you can show the other party that you indeed have excellent composure.

When you are in a serious situation, be proactive in dealing with the issue and in formalizing your communication

If you have regular interaction with a passive-aggressive, you need to make sure that you are being proactive in stopping any serious behavioral patterns that can pose potential damages to you. You should not tolerate negative behaviors from a passive-aggressive person because he will only be encouraged to continue or even exaggerate his negative behaviors. Do not allow the passive-aggressive to set the tone within your relationship. That is your job. As often as possible, make your regular communication with the passive-aggressive formal. You can do this by putting things into writing or by getting other people as your witnesses. Always make sure that you have a paper trail for all issues that you have discussed and for agreements that you have made. When you have agreed on a timeline or specific deadlines, make sure that it is summarized and properly communicated to everyone involved.

When you are in a situation wherein you have to deal with the passive-aggression of a co-worker such as inappropriate jokes or unfulfilled tasks, make sure that you have at least one witness when you discuss the issue with the passive-aggressive colleague. A witness can be anyone who is physically present during your discussion or the appropriate personnel whom you copy in written correspondences. In order to collect information and to let him check the facts, ask a passive-aggressive clarifying or probing questions. Bring out previous emails and other documentations that can support your argument, but make sure that you do not make statements and accusations that start with the word "you" which will only trigger the other person to become defensive. You can opt to start your sentences with "we", "I", "let's" or "it" and then continue with your facts.

Here are examples of ineffective communication: "Your jokes are really distasteful," or "You never meet your deadlines."

Instead of using the above statements, you can opt to simply say "I do not really feel comfortable with the jokes that you say to me. I find them offensive," or "I noted that you were not able to meet the deadline we have agreed on."

If appropriate, allow the passive-aggressive to assist in solving the problem

A lot of passive-aggressive people behave the way they do when they feel that they are not given the chance to voice out their thoughts or to contribute in solving the issue. To address this, allow the passive-aggressive person to become part of the discussions on the issues and their solutions. When appropriate, seek their inputs and suggestions. Appreciate the constructive solutions that they share. But if they only give you criticisms and complaints, don't say anything whether you disagree or agree. You can just tell them that you have noted what they have said and then carry on with your tasks.

To compel cooperation and to reduce resistance from passive-aggressive people, set consequences for both positive and negative behaviors

Many passive-aggressive people operate underhandedly. When someone confronts them on their behavior, they normally create resistance and you will most likely get finger-pointing, excuses and denials from them. But it is advisable not to pay attention to what they tell you. What is important is for you to make your declaration on what you are willing to do to get the results that you want. What you can do is to offer a passive-aggressive a couple of solid consequences that will compel him to reexamine his behaviors.

You will be able to bow out a passive-aggressive by being able to recognize and assert consequences. When you are able to effectively articulate the consequences for specific behaviors, you will be able to let the passive-aggressive to stop and think. He may even be compelled to shift from being obstructive to being cooperative.

Chapter 3: Types Of Difficult People

In both our private and professional lives, we will come across these people. Some might just be a small bother and don't affect our daily life, while others can make us frustrated and angry. These people will seem to be too difficult to deal with, since our personality's clash and nothing seems to get done. However, as you most probably have learnt or will come to learn, we can never escape from difficult people. They are everywhere and the best we can do is to learn how to deal with them. Let's first look at the different types of difficult people.

The bully

These are normally people with very low self-esteem. They make up for this by harassing others and bringing them down so that they can look good themselves. This is what normally happens in learning institutions at all levels. The bullies are normally those students who aren't doing well either academically or in co-curricular activities. They thus have a low self-esteem and to boost it up, they tend to harass other students. They want to gain some recognition and attention that they are not getting through their academic efforts. However, and this might come as a surprise to some, bullying is thriving in the workplace as well. Many employees suffer bullying silently. It may not be outright harassment but occurs in some subtle ways such as some false remarks, some backstabbing, some sarcastic comments and so forth. A boss could also be a bully. They may push you with unrealistic targets and shout at you or hurl abuse which can be interpreted as a form of bullying. When dealing with bullies at any levels, do not show them any fear or signs of intimidation. Make it clear to them that you perceive their behaviors as being bullish and are willing to pursue the matter further. Most bullies are cowards and don't like being hit with the truth. They'll thus retract once they realize you are not falling for their bullish behavior.

The jealous type

This is mostly found in the workplace and at school. Someone feels that you are accomplishing more than them and they can't possibly get to your level. They result to using mediocre tactics such as talking ill of you and trying to undermine your achievements. They can be cunning as they can act very supportive and happy for you but the minute you are out of sight, they fall back to their mediocrity. These kind of people are just jealous and probably do not know what they can do to get to your level. The best way to deal with this kind of personality is to approach them and try helping them in their work so that they don't feel inadequate. You should try complementing them in their efforts so that they don't feel as if they are in competition with you. You'll soon realize that when they concentrate on their work and see good results, they stop their jealousy.

The control freaks

These are the kind of people who always have this need to control everybody around them. They want to know what you are doing and everything in between, even when it doesn't concern them at all. They are usually busy trying to micro manage people even when it's not part of their job and thus their productivity will suffer. Usually this behavior is brought about by anxiety. These people are suffering from a constant state of being anxious and thus feel the need to know what other people are doing. They feel they are always right and tend to be "know it all's". They are quick to blame others when something happens to attempt to justify an earlier held position. With these kinds of people, it's advisable to have an honest chat with them and assure them that everything will be ok and they shouldn't overly mind what everybody else is doing. Make them understand that when everybody concentrates on their job, including them, everything will be fine. These people are often insecure and if you confront them with facts, they back down. They don't want to expose their inadequacies.

The boundary less

There are some people who never understand the concept of boundaries. Most people love their personal space and will often put some form of boundaries in certain areas of their life. If its work, they don't bring their private stuff there. If you are such of a person you'll really get frustrated when someone persistently crosses your boundaries. It will be your responsibility to inform such kind of a person of your boundaries and what they can't cross.

You have to mark your boundaries and back them up by your actions. For instance, you can't say you don't want issues of private life in the workplace yet go ahead and engage in small talk regarding other people's issues.

In the workplace, people can often feel overwhelmed by work demands and feel as if some colleagues are making them do their work. The first step to resolving this would be reading and understanding your job description. You'll then be in a good position to say no to something you feel shouldn't be your responsibility. Communicating clearly and making it clear that you understand your role goes a long way in enforcing your boundaries. People will be hesitant to infringe on them. Lastly saying no is something you need to learn. Many people find it difficult to say no to things they feel uncomfortable about, just because you do not want to seem defiant. You then go on to complain later. Practice saying no and meaning it.

The procrastinator

This is one of the most frustrating traits in a workplace. Procrastination normally reflects some form of resistance. This normally happens when a manager wants something done but somebody is not willing to do it and pushes it away each time. That's why there's the concept of deadline and even so, you'll find most people working hard right on the deadline whereas they had time before. This can result in a shoddy job or a failed project. In school, procrastination can also be a bother when in a group; some person keeps on failing to deliver their part on time. At home too, family members will often feel frustrated when something is not done on time by the responsible party. When people keep on procrastinating, they are not interested in the task at hand and will only do it if they have to. Others will procrastinate to prove they hold the power and want others realize that. A boss at work might delay doing something they have to do, especially affecting their staff to show that they hold the power. In such instances, the best way is to avoid getting into a power struggle. If you are the boss, and your staffs are procrastinating on their work, make them understand that they have responsibilities and the role they play in the success of the team. Communicate to them at every stage to find out what challenge they might be facing. In school or at home, people who procrastinate should be made to understand that they are part of a team and their inactions might adversely affect the rest.

The clinging personalities

These are the kind of people who always want to be taken care off. They are insecure on their own and always need a person they perceive stronger than them to guide them. If it's at work, they don't feel confident or qualified enough to handle a task on their own. If it's at home, they can't trust themselves to make a decision. They feel weak and appear desperate. You can't brush these people off since they'll always come back. The best way is to build their confidence. In most cases, they have the ability to handle most tasks but only lack in confidence. Give them responsibility and show them how to handle a situation on their own.

The competitive types

These are the type of people who are always in competition. They perceive every opportunity as a chance to outshine others. They have this utterly competitive attitude that ultimately affects their colleagues. They have a need to always win. When they don't, they feel an injustice has been served. When dealing with these types of personalities, give them an opportunity to win. Let them bask in the glory but then face them with the facts. They are quick to realize when they were wrong and since they have to protect their self-image, they quickly do what's right without creating a fuss.

Victims

These are people who always feel aggrieved and always blame circumstances for whatever situation they find themselves in. They are passive aggressors. Even when it's clear they are wrong, they will somehow find an excuse or blame it on something. When dealing with these kinds of people don't take their victimization. Be firm with them and show them that it's their own fault and nobody has conspired against them.

Complainers

There are chronic complainers who never see anything good. They will complain about anything and everything without offering a solution. These kinds of people are always bitter. They tend to see others as the course of their own angry state without looking inside themselves. When dealing with such kind of people don't agree with what they say. If they start complaining, try making them look for a solution rather than complain.

Chapter 4: Identifying A Difficult Person

Identifying a Toxic Person

Now, let us look at the defining traits that are common to all types of toxic people. With these traits, you can identify the toxic people in your life and work on getting the toxicity out of your relationship.

Negativity

When anyone in your life is full of negativity, they are undoubtedly toxic. Yes, this trait alone is enough to make someone toxic. This is because of the effects that negativity can have on your life. If someone close to you sees your efforts as being incapable of yielding good results, you need to run from them. Negativity can be related in words, such as when Chloe told Nancy she was not cut out for law even though Nancy had won the award of best associate in the firm. Negativity can also come in deeds, such as when your brother, who had the opportunity to support you, refused to because he thought you were bound to fail in your endeavor, with no solid reason.

Envious

This is something that goes on in the mind but it may eventually leak through the cracks of the impulsive actions of the envious one, especially towards the envied. When, upon receiving a gift from your boyfriend, you caught an expressionless look on your friend's face, that may be the clue you need. When someone envies you for having something they do not have, their reaction to you will be that of scorn disguised as constructive criticism. Envy can serve as a very effective trigger for toxicity.

Humiliation

Humiliation, as a weapon in the arsenal of a toxic person, is employed when they try to be in control. If you prove yourself capable of seeing through them, through their ruse and façade, they will try to strip you of any dignity. This is to show you are no better than they are. Do not be surprised when they publicly use something you told them in confidence, against you, the same way John had used his knowledge of Bryan's medical history against him in a bar.

Domineering

As a feature of toxic people, expect them to want to lord it over you. It is an insatiable craving of theirs. Even when you stoop to the lowliest of points for them, they still are not satisfied. You need to be at their beck and call, to serve them, to satisfy them, to inconvenience yourself for them. If they are your boss, they have little regard for your dignity and overburden you with work, giving you the craziest of deadlines. These are deadlines that even they in their usual 'I-was-once-where-you-are-now" attitude cannot possibly meet. They want to feel in control and ensure they never lose grip on you.

Manipulative

This can come directly or indirectly. When it is direct, they appeal to your empathy, such as sobbing, crying, or emphasizing how much of a problem there will be if you do not do their bidding. When it is indirect, they appeal to your ego, your desire to be recognized and praised by them. They flatter you and put you on a high horse to nowhere. They string you out and leave you to dry.

Opportunistic

You are in business, and things are not going well for you. The banks have just called in the loans and all your assets, when sold, cannot even cover the interest, let alone the principal. You decide to initiate bankruptcy proceedings, but there is one concern: your mother's house used as collateral for the loan will be sold. You want that rich friend to buy the house, hold in some trust, and sell it back to you when things are good again. Of course, he has the means to even gift it to you. He agrees to it, and you facilitate his buying it. But when the time comes for him to transfer it back to you, he reneges on his promise. This friend is opportunistic. They secretly wish for your misfortune so that they can profit from it. Your case may not be a loan. It can be something as simple as their trying to take a position they knew you were wrongfully denied rather than trying to help you get it back.

Aggressive

Here, you must recall the bar fight between John and Bryan. The toxic people in your life resort to threats and force to get what they want from you or any other person. They are grown-up bullies whose desire to dominate other individuals forces them to do more than manipulate you. When you have suffered physical harm from a friend even once in unjustified aggression, the chances are that they are toxic and you should flee from them. The next time, you may not live to remember what happened, let alone reflect on it.

Sadistic and Unsympathetic

Some people enjoy being cruel to you just for fun. They derive pleasure from all the physical and mental torture they inflict on you. It pleases them to see you in pain, in anguish. They know, and they do not feel sorry for it, not even when you confront them about it. They keep coming back to you because they find you easy prey. Why go in search of another victim when here is the perfect one, you? These people are also insulated from feeling pity for you or from being able to imagine themselves in your shoes. They cannot do any of those because to them, it would be a sign of weakness.

Lying and Exaggerating

As a feature of toxicity, the borderline between these two, lying and exaggerating, becomes blurred. I am saying you find it difficult to tell when they are saying the truth because even when they are, they overstate it for reasons of invoking your pity or gaining your heightened admiration. Their lies can hurt you, mentally and physically: they make it difficult for you to trust them, to rely on them. Their exaggeration can confuse you, forcing you to act rashly. The simple truth is that they have no place in your life.

Form Rather than Substance

This is the toxic person's best way to wiggle out of ugly situations. They pay attention to form rather than substance. Imagine Ridley trying to discredit the two research papers because the publishers publish too many works yearly to be able to pay close attention to what they are publishing. Or imagine Chloe telling Nancy that if indeed she, Chloe, had done anything wrong, Nancy's reaction had made them even. All Nancy had said was, 'Chloe, I think we need to talk about us. I feel like we are not of great benefit to each other.'

The people in your life can possess any of the above traits to varying degrees. Any single one of them may be sufficient to declare someone as toxic. But pause a little bit. Why do you think you have toxic people in your life? Why do you find it difficult to evaluate any of your relationships and not find a John, a Ridley, or a Charlie in it? Could you be the problem? Could the problem be something else?

Chapter 5: Empathise And Neutralise

Step 3 focuses on the importance of being empathetic and neutralising the situation as this will help to defuse the situation. You need to be genuinely empathetic to the other person's emotions AND you need to acknowledge their emotions. Create an atmosphere that shows you care.

Here's what you need to do and this part of the process is ABSOLUTELY CRUCIAL: Allow the angry person to vent.

Whilst the angry person is venting, your role is to listen. Listen and listen some more –Even if you have heard the same story before, you must allow the angry person to vent whilst your role is to listen!

Have you read "The 7 Habits of Highly Effective People" by Steven Covey? It's a best selling book and well worth reading if you haven't done so yet. Habit No 5 is to 'Seek first to understand and then to be understood'. Seek first to understand: put yourself in the other person's shoes and try to see things from their viewpoint. Wow, such valuable advice.

When you take the time to truly listen to the other person, they in turn are going to be far more prepared to reciprocate and listen to what it is you have to say and to be influenced by you.

During this early stage DO NOT...

interrupt

disagree

blame

excuse

explain

defend yourself

mind read or second guess what the person is going to say

confuse issues with personalities

During the venting stage it is not uncommon for the angry person to be interrupted by the listener, especially if the listener totally disagrees with what is being said.

The desire to voice your thinking can be overwhelming, I know, but this is a No-No! This will only antagonise them further. An angry person does not want to listen to excuses, or blame, they just want their problem fixed. Once the antagonist has calmed down, THEN you can share your thinking.

It's time for active listening. Truly listen. Pay attention to what they are saying, search for the underlying reasons for their upset, what their version of the facts are, what an acceptable solution would be for them. Pay attention also to their body language, and what they perhaps are choosing NOT to tell you.

Your attention and focus needs to be on understanding the angry person. You need to suspend all judgment and be as understanding as possible. Validating phrases work really well here – it sends a message that you are truly listening. You could say "that's interesting, tell me more' or "so what you are saying is that…".

Aim to find some way to agree. It helps to create 'common ground'.

Empathetic Listening And Clarifying Questions

Empathetic Listening is the doorway to re-building the relationship. When you practise empathetic listening the focus is NOT on you, it is on the other person.

Empathetic statements allow you to reflect the angry person's message back to them in a non-confrontation way. It allows you to capture their emotions and concerns and frustrations and do so without you needing to agree or disagree. Everyone has a right to feel the way they do and to their own point of view.

Here's a great suggestion for you. Start the empathetic statements with the wording: "So You…" So You puts the focus on THE OTHER PERSON.

The angry person says: "This is the third time you've simply ignored my request for some help".

You reply: "I understand your frustration. So you feel that I'm ignoring you and your needs when I don't help."

It's also time for clarifying questions, so as to better understand their concerns and what they are wanting.

"In what way was the quality inferior to what you expected?"

"What do you believe would be a fairer way of handling this?"

"Let's see if I've understood your concern…". Then paraphrase

The Importance Of Allowing The Disgruntled Person To Vent

To illustrate the importance of giving the angry person time to vent, I'm going to share a story with you.

Several years ago I gave a seminar for an organisation whose role it is to police the payment of royalties when a certain product was used by businesses; most often small to medium sized businesses. For the purpose of this story, I'll give this organisation a fictitious name: "Royalty Collections Pty Ltd".

This organization would send our invoices twice yearly, and they knew from experience that soon after they would be flooded with phone calls from angry business owners, many of when did not even realize they would need to pay a royalty to use this particular product, and they would fiercely object.

The customer service staff of the organisation would receive these calls and needed to handle them. They pretty much knew what the caller was going to say, as they'd heard the same story and concerns over and over again, so instead of listening and allowing the caller to vent, they would move the conversation forward and suggest a solution. The solution usually was that the caller could either:

Stop using the product

Or maybe use it less often and so be charged a lesser fee

An agreement was usually finally reached, however the caller was usually still pretty angry about the unexpected expense.

Royalty Collections Pty ltd wanted to develop a better relationship with their customers whilst still offering them the same two options as a solution. During the course of my training we discussed the need for the customer service staff to allow the caller to 'vent'. Regardless of how many times the customer service person had heard the same concerns, they still had to listen to each disgruntled business person, they still had to express empathy, apologize, ask clarifying questions, use paraphrasing statements, and not try to move the conversation forward too soon.

The customer service staff put into practice my recommendations and the feedback was that the new approach was working really well. The customers were far more prepared to discuss the situation and staff stress levels decreased considerably. Whilst the callers were not necessarily 'happy' about having to pay a royalty they were far more understanding and accepting of the situation and no longer furious by the end of the phone conversation.

Don't respond with anger

Every single one of us needs to have emotional management strategies that we can call on that will help us to manage our emotions when faced with an angry person. It can be destructive to speak in the heat of the moment. Here are some ideas that work for lots of people:

Counting to 10 works for some people

Engaging in deep-breathing is also popular as it helps one to stay relaxed

Change one's thinking can also work – remember, perception is reality

Have a drink of water

Remove emotion when you speak, so normal pace and don't raise the pitch of your voice

If you can feel anger escalating then it is probably time to postpone the conversation. It's time for "Time Out". In other words, time to suspend the conversation until such time as you are more in control of your emotions. This strategy is equally effective if it is the other person who needs to gain emotional control.

When postponing the conversation …

ALWAYS suggest a date and time to meet again

Provide a couple of meeting time options for

the other person to choose from

When you give them choices, as opposed to 'telling' them when you wish to meet again, you are inviting the other party to decide. So you are giving them a sense of ownership, which is good.

Graceful Exit Lines

Whenever a discussion gets heated, it is difficult to have a sensible conversation when the parties concerned are attacking and playing the blame game instead of focusing on finding a solution. So trying to continue the discussion when the other person is truly angry may only add fuel to the fire. The same principle applies if it is you who is getting upset.

In either case, a sensible alternative is to give the angry participant(s) time to calm down by delaying the conversation until later. This is what I call "Taking Time Out".

Suggesting 'time out' often requires a degree of diplomacy. A good strategy is to use what I have been taught to call "graceful exit lines". A graceful exit line is simple a phrase you can use to gracefully exit and postpone the conversation.

I've put together some examples for you of graceful exit lines. Here they are:

"Let me gather all the facts and we can then get back together."

"I appreciate how very important this is to you. Can we schedule time for this discussion when I can give it my full attention?"

"I have a meeting shortly. I can make myself available …………… or …………."

" I'll need a few minutes to check on that."

"It's obvious we both feel strongly about this. How about we take a break and continue this discussion later?"

"Let's each do our homework and re-convene within the next 24 hours."

"Give me a few hours to get to the bottom of this."

"I would like to gather my thoughts as to how we can resolve this as quickly as possible."

"Let me get back to you on that."

"How about we take time out to get some fresh air. I need to clear my head."

PLEASE NOTE:

For any one of these examples to work for you, you need to also suggest a couple of specific times (and maybe a location) to get back together. Give the other party choices and a say in the matter by providing a couple of options. For example:

"Can we get back together this afternoon at 3pm or would you prefer tomorrow at 10am?"

"I'm dropping my daughter off at sport at 4pm, would any time after that suit you to continue our conversation?"

"After my meeting, I am free for the rest of the day, what time would best suit you to catch up?"

Chapter 6: Why Dealing With Stress Is Important For Dealing With Difficult People

No one likes dealing with difficult people, but sometimes the task is required. In order to handle difficult people, you need to be in control of yourself and your stress level first. For people in high stress jobs such as retail, taking the time to relax and re-center themselves can help provide the emotional energy for dealing with such individuals. People who do not take the time to refresh and recharge themselves may not be able to handle stressful situations of any kind as well as they otherwise would.

Effects of Stress

Stress is a serious issue that has physical, mental and emotional consequences. It can never be entirely avoided because it is a normal reaction to dealing with difficult situations in everyday life. However, it can be dealt with by taking time to consciously relax.

The effects of stress are cumulative to a certain extent. People who work in stressful environments all week are usually much more stressed out on Thursday than on Monday. The weekend provides a chance to rest and recover that the shorter, overnight break between workdays does not offer.

Stress and Emotional Energy

Everyone has had a moment in their lives where they just could not deal with a situation any longer. Usually, the reaction to reaching this point is quite dramatic, involving yelling, tears, or stomping off in a huff. In most cases, it is not the specific situation that caused the person to reach their breaking point, but the amount of emotional energy they had when they got into the situation. People have longer "fuses" when they are under less stress. Individuals each have their own unique ability to deal with emotionally stressful situations and some are naturally more tolerant of them than others. However, anyone can increase their ability to deal with stressful situations by consciously relieving stress.

Reactions to Difficult People

The opposite reaction to the dramatic "breaking point" screaming or crying is to shut down. This often happens when people are involved in stressful situations within their own families or in other areas of life where they cannot get away. Shutting down can lead to making unhealthy decisions simply to please the difficult person. This is because making the healthier decision would require fighting and fighting requires energy. Relieving stress can allow people in these situations to build up their reserves and fight for their own needs to be met. It takes more emotional energy initially but can result in a better situation overall.

People who find themselves shutting down may need to remove themselves from the situation until they have recharged their batteries. Then they can fight for their needs.

Relieving Stress

Ways of relieving stress are unique to individuals. What one person finds lowers their stress level might actually increase the stress level of another individual. Some common activities that people use for stress relief include physical exertion, social gatherings, quiet time spent with friends and family, creative endeavors and much more. Generally, anything that leaves someone feeling more relaxed when they are finished than when they began can be considered a method of stress relief.

As you deal with difficult people at work or in the home, be aware of your own stress levels. If you sense that you are under a lot of stress, remove yourself from the situation. Ask someone else for help to deal with the difficult person so you can reduce your stress and regain your emotional energy. Being calm within yourself is the first step towards successfully dealing with difficult people.

Chapter 7: Attitude Transfer

Transfer may result worse or Better

Attitude Transfer

To further understand the mechanics of being a difficult person, it is

necessary to know that some attitudes may be transferred, and any such

transfer may result in a worse or better attitude.

It is a law of nature. Good cells always produce better, healthier cells. Bad cells produce worse cells, and worse cells produce dead cells later. A good tree produces good fruits, and a bad tree produces bad crops.

Now, by putting the pressure reversal to work, the vicious cycle can be

interrupted and can produce the exact opposite:

• A good attitude can spring up from a bad attitude if the bearer

simply decides to be different and works it out.

• A bad tree may be treated with reversal treatments like grafting

and spraying to make it bear good fruits.

A difficult person is difficult probably because he got it from someone

close to him:

• A difficult father may inadvertently transfer his personality to a

child who either idolizes or abhors him.

•A professor may transfer his attitude to his students.

•You may acquire the characteristics of your friends.

Hero-worship Transfer

When a successful person is a difficult person, those who idolize him

and follow in his footsteps may also turn out to be difficult individuals

too. They will see that a factor in his success is his dealing with people.

People always attribute their success partly to management skill.

To others, management skills equate to how you talk to and treat people;

or worse, putting pressure on people for them to work harder.

Likewise, a person who ends up in tragedy may appear successful to

others as a hero because he personifies a cause they are fighting for.

For example, a janitor, while trying to save his boss, dies in a fire. He may be idolized by his sons who would also become janitors loyal to their bosses.

It is good to emulate really good heroes, but even difficult people can

appear heroes to some people, and thus people imitate their attitude.

Dictators have always left behind followers that may become even more

ruthless.

Abhorrence transfer

World history is replete with people who deposed dictators only to become worse dictators themselves.

There are two reasons for the transfer of this attitude:

1. Revenge.

Some people who suffered at the hands of difficult people

tend to repeat everything to their subordinates or to the next generation.

Here works the Principle of Substitution.

Imagine a rebel group overthrowing an oppressive

government, with a new leader installed as the head of state.

The quest for revenge would logically be taken out on those

deposed.

But imagine that they are now dead, or have fled the country

and are no longer reachable, perhaps being protected by another government.

The new leader may then take out his revenge on those under

him who are powerless.

Those under him become substitutes for the real object of

vengeance.

Hence, the child who suffers from his difficult father might

release his frustration on his younger brother

The younger brother might take on his pet dog.

2. Holding on to power.

Imagine a sales manager who hates his difficult boss, who

has the title of sales director.

The difficulty stems, in part, from the director taking credit

for the sales of his subordinate, the sales manager. He does this in an effort to maintain his position of power.

Then a change takes place and the sales manager is promoted

to the position of sales director, replacing his former boss. He begins to love the position so much that he understands the attitude of his ex boss and soon proves to be as difficult, or more difficult, than his predecessor.

He is a victim of a difficult person and hates it.

But he then becomes a more severe copy of the person who

made life so difficult for him. Why? It is because he wants to hold onto power.

Chapter 8: How To Handle Gossip And Workplace Bullies

How to Handle Gossip in the Workplace

Gossips are a natural part of any workplace. Place people in one room together for several hours per day, several days per week and word is bound to be spread. If you're the boss and you find yourself addressing gossip issues more frequently than you'd care to, then the first step would be to determine whether

the gossip is affecting work productivity

the gossip is damaging an employee's emotions or his reputation

the gossip is causing social discord in the workplace

the gossip is hurting a worker's morale

If such is the case, then action is required.

☐ The first thing to do would be to evaluate yourself as a boss and determine whether you are sharing enough information with your workers. Often gossip is a result of over-speculation due to not having enough facts to hold onto.

☐ Manage gossiping employees by utilizing the coaching approach.

☐ If necessary, initiate a three-way conversation involving you, the employee, and the supervisor. You may start by giving a verbal warning. If the problem continues, write a formal warning to be kept in the worker's personal file.

☐ You may encourage a gossip-free work environment by enforcing the rule in your company policy.

☐ Set an example for your subordinates. Don't belittle yourself by participating in gossip.

☐Maintain open communication lines. If your employees feel like they can't talk to you, they end up complaining amongst themselves. To minimize gossip in the office, practice some transparency.

☐Don't shoot the messenger. If you punish every employee that brings in bad news, you will end up discouraging other employees. And then they're more likely to huddle together, whispering amongst themselves.

But what if you end up as the victim of these vicious rumors?

☐ Confront the person spreading the gossip. Let them know that you're on to what they're doing. This may put an end to the gossip. If the rumor involves another person, then mention that you are willing to verify the story with that other person.

☐When confronting people about gossips, you should deal with the rumors and not with the person. Display professionalism by saying: "I am concerned about the rumors spreading about me. I want it to end." instead of saying: "You're a terrible person. Stop spreading nasty stuff about me."

☐ Generally, a clear and simple denial is enough to smother and kill groundless gossip.

☐ The normal response to people whispering behind your back would be to act defensively. However, you should avoid this. One thing that you can do is to approach your coworkers in a conversational tone and mention that you've been hearing some rumors about you floating around the office. You don't need to mention names. Then, state that if anyone has any questions about you, you are open for a conversation anytime.

☐ One of the most common subjects of gossip is romantic relationships in the workplace. If there is truth to the matter and if dating someone in the office does not violate any company policies, then come clean and clarify that there are no conflicts.

☐ When you find out that someone is spreading a rumor about you, you need not necessarily be aggressive in your confrontation. One thing you can do is to approach the person and tell him how terribly concerned you are about these false rumors. Then, ask for his help to shut down the rumors.

☐ Don't participate in gossip. Keep in mind that people who gossip to you are also likely to gossip about you. Either you avoid or ignore the person or you may change the subject in a subtle manner. If it's not possible to shift the focus of the conversation, then try to verify the facts by asking questions. This should put an end to a gossiper who's not able to supply details.

☐ Lastly, there's no need to act all self-righteous. This is likely to turn workmates against you. If you feel like people are gossiping and complaining too much, redirect their attention and their energies by offering solutions instead.

How to Handle Bullies in the Workplace

☐ Establish limits.

Be clear on what you will and will not tolerate from the bully. However, more than that exercise your right to tell your coworker to stop the behavior.

Describe the behavior. There's no need to expound on the topic or to add in your opinions. Just state exactly what you see the bully doing.

Ex.: "You enter my cubicle frequently, uninvited. You pick up papers from my desk without so much as asking me and then you read them."

Then, inform your co-worker exactly how his actions are affecting your work.

Ex.: "Most of my work is confidential and because of this behavior, I am forced to feel as though I need to conceal my work from you. That's very stressful. Furthermore, arranging and rearranging the papers on my desk is very time-consuming on my part.

Afterwards, inform your co-worker that you will no longer put up with his bullying behavior in the future.

Ex.: "For future references, you are not to enter my cubicle again uninvited. As long as you continue with this behavior, you will not be welcome in my private work space."

Lastly, have the courage to stick to your statements. If it doesn't work out then the next step would be to confront the bully with his behavior.

☐ Confront your bullying co-worker with his own conduct.

The thing about bullies is that they're only good when they're standing on firm ground. Therefore, the best thing that you can do is to take the ground away from that bully. The next time your coworker calls you a nasty name, call his behavior out. It's not too different from dealing with a child throwing a fit. As an adult, you shouldn't give in to the bully's tantrums because this will encourage more outbursts.

You may also employ this confrontational approach for coworkers who have a tendency to talk over you in meetings. The next time he points out your mistakes, ask him directly what he can suggest instead. If it doesn't work out, you can tell your coworker that he's free to leave the meeting until you are done with your presentation. If he refuses to do this, gauge if it's possible for you to reorganize the meeting with the exclusion of your colleague.

☐ Practice documentation.

Whenever you experience bullying in the workplace, record the details of the incident. Be sure to document the time and the date as well. This way, in case you decide to approach the HR department for help, then you'll have documentation that your coworker is negatively impacting your work progress. If the bullying is performed via email, then print a hard copy of the conversation. It may require witnesses in order for the management to make the necessary actions. If there are any other coworkers who are or have been a target of this person's bullying, then ask them to document their experiences as well. That way, you'll be able to build a strong case when you get to the HR. Check your employee handbook and acquaint yourself with your company's anti-bullying policy.

Chapter 9: Why People Are Difficult

Causes of Conflict

There are many reasons why conflicts arise between you and other people. These conflicts are what make people so difficult. Often, you get along with someone just fine until your needs or views start to conflict. Then, you realize that this person poses a hardship or hurdle of some sort for you. You must understand the cause of conflict in order to go about solving these conflicts. Once you solve conflicts, you will find that a majority of difficult people suddenly become easier to deal with.

Four Intents

There are four intents that commonly lead to conflict. These intents are where you may run into difficulties when dealing with other people.

The first intent is to get a task done. You want to get something done. Other people may or may not care about getting it done. You can run into some conflict trying to get other people to focus on working with you to get a task done.

The second intent is to get the task done right. People are apt to have their own ideas about how everything should be done. As a result, you will run into a lot of disagreement on how to get a task done right.

The third intent is to get along with people. Most people share this intent in theory. But when it comes to practice, many people have no clue to all get along. People all have different needs and communication styles. This can make getting along difficult as everyone conflicts.

The fourth and final intent is to earn the appreciation and recognition of others for your efforts. You are likely to run into a lot of conflict here. Not everyone is going to appreciate you or your work. If they do, they may express their appreciation in odd ways. Some people may be jealous of you or angry with you, so they refuse to acknowledge something that you have done well. Similarly, you may make others resentful when you do not provide the recognition that they desire. Lack of recognition is likely to create a lot of conflict.

Lack of Communication

A lack of communication is the most common root of conflict. If someone becomes difficult, you are probably not communicating well. You both get frustrated as you misinterpret each other. You get insulted over things that were not intended to be insulting, you develop groundless expectations, and you create delays and discord. Clear communication is essential to resolving conflict. I will cover clear communication tips later in Chapter 5.

Differences

Different ideals can make you not get along well with a person. You may have different ideals about lifestyle, work, religion, philosophy, or ethics. You may have different goals in life that do not mix together well. Whenever you experience a difference of preference or opinion with someone, you face the possibility of conflict.

It is important to be understanding that other people are not the same as you. Be sensitive to differences in backgrounds, cultures, and opinions. You should let go of conflicts where you are trying to change or convince someone to see things your way. This is just not a reasonable or useful endeavor. You will probably just wind up frustrated.

It is also important to stick to your own guns. You have the right to lead life as you see fit, and you should be firm in your decisions. You do not have to explain yourself or lie about yourself, you just have to be firm and resolute. Your firmness will end a lot of the meddling. When it doesn't, you can politely ask them to leave you be and stop trying to deviate you from your goals.

Fear

Fear is a common cause of conflict. People will fight you if they feel that you pose any sort of danger to them. The danger does not have to be a physical threat. If you threaten someone's comfort and routine, you can stir up a vicious reaction. People are fiercely defensive of their comfort and will refuse to work with you if you pose a threat to their normal way of life or of doing things.

If you bring change with you, you will scare people. People will become difficult as they fight to maintain their routines. Try showing people how change will benefit them so that they become more accepting of the tides of change that you bring. Sometimes, you should just not try to fix something that is not broken. In other words, if the change you bring is not truly necessary, why expend so much effort to force it on people who do not welcome it? Consider that you might be the cause of peoples' difficult behavior if you are trying to force useless change on others.

Pride

A cause of most conflict is probably pride. Pride lies at the bottom of stubborn and difficult behavior. People refuse to bend to you because of pride, so they act in difficult ways. You may also engage in pride and refuse to bend as well. As a result, everyone behaves in a difficult way and nothing is accomplished.

Pride can be a useful emotion. But it is best in small, healthy doses. Recognize when your pride is getting you nowhere.

Drop your pride in favor of a good solution. When it comes to others' pride, try to avoid hurting their pride and offer them lots of benefits for working with you.

Reasons People Act Difficult

If someone is particularly challenging, you might want to consider why. It is always a good idea to be empathetic in all areas of life. By being empathetic, you can pinpoint and thus address the cause of someone's difficult behavior. You can find some sort of solution that works out well for everyone. There are many different reasons for why people act in difficult ways, beyond the causes of conflict that I discussed above. Consider these different reasons if you are running into problems with someone.

Bad Day

People can be difficult or rude when they are having a bad day. Consider that people who snap at you or treat you badly may just be at their wits' end. They may be tired, hungry, and crabby so they are not willing to be nice and easygoing. A person who does not feel well for health or emotional reasons will probably be difficult.

Try to be more sympathetic and understanding. Do not take someone's random outbursts of rudeness or difficult behavior personally. It is likely unrelated to you. Usually, when someone acts out, it is for their own personal reasons. You can try to communicate and ask them what is wrong, or you can just ignore the behavior and move on with your life.

Unintentional Rudeness

A lot of the time, people do not intend to be rude. For whatever reason, someone may act rudely without even meaning to be rude. Try not to take rudeness so personally and understand that there may be legitimate reasons behind this rude behavior. Do not let someone's behavior determine who that person is for you. People often are not their behavior.

Rudeness may be bred out of habit. People who have been raised in rude families or who have not been reprimanded for their rude behavior before may continue to act rudely without even realizing how hurtful their behavior is. These people will often be shocked and even confused when confronted.

It can be caused by cultural differences. These differences may be as small as regional cultural differences. Someone may be rude to you because he or she is simply acting in a way that is normal to his or her native culture. Some cultures do not believe in smiling, for instance. Other cultures may be brusque or may be open to asking what Americans deem as invasive questions. If someone is not from your area, consider that a cultural difference is at play.

Disabilities can also lead to rudeness. Some people suffer from social anxiety and are not able to follow conventional social rules in public because they are so nervous. They are desperate to get away from you and may not respond to things that you say or may appear to avoid you. People suffering from Asperger's or other disorders on the autism spectrum are also unable to follow conventional social norms. If someone acts oddly around you, do not become offended or confront them. Instead, consider that something is wrong. Not all disorders are starkly visible to the naked eye, so reserve judgment and hurt.

Then it is perfectly possible that someone is simply unaware that he or she is being rude. People who are in a hurry or preoccupied with something else may inadvertently treat you rudely. People who have not been taught any better while growing up may also act out in rude ways, without intending any harm.

When someone is rude, consider that he or she did not mean to be. You do not have to get all upset over someone's rudeness. Stop wasting so much emotional energy on people that have little importance in your life. Their lack of manners may have been unintentional. Even if they mean to be rude, you do not have to let it affect your day.

Lack of Respect

Deliberate rudeness, deceit, manipulation, and underhandedness all serve as glaring signs that someone has no respect for you. People who disrespect you will not take you seriously. They will not mind hurting you and violating your boundaries. The difficulties that they pose for you are bred out of their lack of caring for your well-being.

When you realize that someone disrespects you, you can either walk away or present someone with consequences for his or her disrespectful treatment of you. Do not tolerate disrespect. Offer a serious punishment to those who do not treat you right. Sometimes the best punishment is to withdraw your affection and leave the scene.

Opposing Views

A person who views something differently from you will pose a huge difficulty for you. He or she will work to erect boundaries in order to satisfy his or her own goals and block yours. He or she may also try to tell you what to do and change your course of action or your beliefs.

You can work with such people by offering a compromise. Discuss your opposing views and make it clear that you are not interested in changing yourself or the other person. Agree to disagree. This is impossible for some people, so walk away from such people.

Insecurities and Jealousy

Insecure people tend to get jealous. And jealous people are often hateful. A jealous person will be the worst enemy that you ever have. He or she will constantly work to hurt, undermine, and discredit you. His or her goal in life will be to bring you down, so he or she deliberately targets you all of the time. A jealous person will pose many difficulties for you.

Jealousy often arises when someone is threatened by you and perceives that you possess something he or she wishes to have. Whether this is success, a romantic partner, looks, money, or a valued possession, you will encounter difficulties deliberately created by this person. You can identify people who envy you by their unexplained, intense hatred and their apparent obsession with ruining your life.

Deal with envy maturely. Take it as a compliment. Then try to communicate with someone who is jealous of you with great kindness. Tell him or her how to get whatever you have that is so coveted. You can kill this kind of difficulty with kindness.

Revenge

Vindictiveness also can make a person become difficult for you to deal with. Someone who has it out for you will prove to be a formidable enemy. Consider if you have made any enemies somehow. Is there a reason that this person may hate you? Do you two have prior history?

If you find that someone may desire revenge on you, then apologize for your wrongdoing and offer a reasonable solution. Try to make things right. Prove your innocence if you did nothing wrong. Open communication is often the best solution to this issue.

Chapter 10: Fight Only The Battles Worth Fighting

It is no secret that negative and difficult people are everywhere. You're going to see them everywhere you look. Most likely, you're going to encounter them at every point in your life. However, even if that is so, it doesn't mean that you always have to confront them.

Keep in mind that majority of them will not stay long in your life. In fact, they're just going to pass by. This means that they're going to make your life miserable only for a few minutes, hours or days at most. When dealing with such people, it's best to keep your composure and let them pass by as fast as possible.

For example, you're on the phone with the meanest and worst possible customer service rep ever. In this case, you have two choices. Your first choice is to go on with the call and try to explain your problem.

The second is to just drop the call and call another agent, which hopefully will be better. The latter is an approach that I highly recommend because it doesn't allow other people to have power over you, at least, not for a long time. That's exactly what you should do all the time.

Another thing that you have to remember is that not all difficult people are in your life to bring you down. In fact, it's just that they're difficult to deal with. However, if you see past all their difficulties, you will see that they have a few positive qualities as well. For example, imagine a financial analyst, who although being quite a bitch (sorry for the lack of a better word), has a lot of things to bring to your team. Sure, she's difficult to deal with most of the time, but you have to remember that you'll need her every now and then.

To put it simply, some people are worth dealing with and worth the patience. You may find yourself losing quite a few hours of sleep because of them and you may even be throwing little tantrums in private because of how they get on your nerves. But remember, if this were a fight, you'd be losing because of how you let other people get on your nerves.

So, make sure that you always think twice and only fight the battles that are worth fighting.

Learn How to Communicate Effectively

Not everyone is born with strong problem solving skills. However, that doesn't mean that you can't learn them. In fact, throughout our life, it's important to spend time every now and then to try to become a better problem solver.

The reason for this is that people with excellent problem solving skills are good with people as well. They also make for great leaders, have more harmonious relationships with people, get better cooperation from their teammates and most important of all, they gain the respect of everyone around them.

The question now is, how do you become an excellent problem solver?

For starters, you have to know how to separate the issue from the person. By doing this, you're able to be soft on the person you're dealing with, but tough when tackling the issue.

For example, a conversation may go like this:

"I want the both of us to talk, but I can't do that when you're angry. Either we can keep our cool and be more calm about things or we can go out for a while and come back to talk about this later. Your choice."

Or alternatively, like this:

"I appreciate you working so hard for me these past few days. However, you're still behind with your projects. I was hoping to talk about how we can improve that so that you finish your jobs on time."

Remember, when we're soft on the people we're dealing with, they become more open to what we have to say. When people are more open, they're likely to improve and do better the next time around.

Now, isn't that what you want to happen? Don't you want your flunking student to stop getting Fs on every exam and get at least Cs the next time around?

The next time you're dealing with people, always remember this phrase: "firm on the issue, soft on the person."

Talk about Them

Difficult people deal with things differently. Instead of talking about the problem and solving it, they're quick to point out what's wrong. This is exactly what makes them so difficult to deal with, since this doesn't really solve anything.

The reason why they do this is that they want to make you feel insecure. They want you to feel bad about yourself, and when you do, they feel a bit better about themselves and get rid of some of their own insecurities.

You'll encounter a lot of these people everyday, and even more so at work. The best way to deal with them is to avoid being defensive. If you're defensive, they'll likely scrutinize you. Whenever you let other people do this to you, you give them power OVER YOU.

The quickest and best way to avoid this is to put the spotlight back on them. Instead of letting yourself be the topic of the conversation, try and slingshot everything back to them.

For example, the conversation can go like this:

Difficult Person: "What you're doing isn't even close to what I asked you to do."

You: "Did you ever stop to think about what exactly it is that you want me to do?"

Difficult Person: "You're just so stupid. You know?"

You: "Keep on doing that and you're not going to have someone working for you anymore. I'm pretty sure you don't want that. Just let me know what exactly it is that you want and I'll do it for you. If you can't, then I'll gladly go."

As you can see, this isn't a defensive way of doing things. It's more of an aggressive approach, but where you still keep an open mind about things.

By keeping the spotlight on the difficult person, you help neutralize their negativity, and in turn, you negate their effect on you.

Chapter 11: Change Your Behavior

The second strategy is to change your behavior towards difficult people. Your difficult counterpart may discover that his or her behavior places you at a disadvantage. He or she will then use this tactic to get what they want. To avoid this, change how you deal with the person, which will force that person to learn new ways of dealing with you.

In simple terms, you should never let difficult people get the upper hand. To do this, you have to learn how to cope with different types of difficult counterparts.

How to change your behavior and the way you act towards different types of difficult people

We are going to consolidate the six types of difficult people we looked at in the first chapter into three categories; then, we are going to outline how to change your behavior and act towards each category.

The Aggressor Type

These types of difficult people believe they need to demonstrate tough actions and behavior to get things done their way. In your work place, you and other colleagues tolerate these types of colleagues because they are productive. They normally get things done. This type of person can be your highly ranked boss or supervisor. The way they affect your ability and those of your colleagues to get work done gives them an edge.

However, their behavior might be distractive and negative to you and others around you. That is why it is important to know how to deal with them.

How to deal with aggressors

Only address the issue at hand

Aggressors have one very irritating character: They normally approach you with an issue and then blow it out of proportion by bringing up other related issues. When this happens, it is very easy to lose focus on the issue at hand. You can rectify this annoying situation by addressing the key issue. This will help you avoid confusion.

You can use phrases like "let's focus on the key point for now please". Saying this as calmly and as frequent as necessary will cause the aggressor to refocus on the topic.

Exercise active listening

Aggressive people normally talk a lot. This process may sometime result in abuse or disrespect. You should not take this personally. Just hold your thoughts and try to listen without responding. Your aggressor may actually have a point; therefore, you must remain objective to what he or she is saying. Obviously, this will help you understand the difficult person and avoid an argument by not taking things personally.

Hold your ground

Never let an aggressor change your view or position on something. Aggressors are very intimidating; if you are not strong enough, they will try to bully you into seeing things their way. When you hold your ground on an issue, the aggressor will learn you are not a pushover, which will discourage bad behavior towards you. However, if you let the person intimidate you, you will have supported the bad behavior; the person will feel convinced that bullying gets results, which will encourage him or her to use the method whenever he or she is dealing with you. The power is in your hands.

Seek a win-win situation

The best way to diffuse an aggressor is by being polite and respectful as you hold your ground. You can co-exist with an aggressor by seeking a win-win situation. A good example of this is an instance where an aggressor tries to force a wrong idea. In this instance, you can respond by saying, "I hear what you are saying and you have some very compelling points, but we and the team have determined that the best way forward is…and we want you to become part of the team, even if you are not a supporter of this plan."

Always control your emotions

When you are dealing with an aggressor, you should always keep your emotions under control because being over emotional only adds wood to the fire. Aggressors are naturally rude and love arguing. When you start counter attacking them, you will be playing their game and you will lose. You might even say something that you will regret later. So save yourself some embarrassment and keep your emotions under control.

Do not embarrass them

One of the major rules of dealing with an aggressor is never to embarrass him or her in front of people because the embarrassment tends to escalate their undesired behavior, causing them to develop defensive reactions towards you.

The Victim Type

Victims are the type of difficult people who never seem to accomplish anything. They instead hide themselves in piles of excuses. When they do not accomplish their goals, they shift blame to you or circumstances. They normally say things like, "I didn't have information to back me up," or "It's not my fault". Their characters include always feeling sorry for themselves, blaming others, appearing helpless, and blowing things out of proportion.

How to Deal with Victim Type of People

Focus on solutions

When you are dealing with a victim, only communicate solutions. Tell them what they can do differently next time and what you expect from them in the future. If you do not do this, they will suck you into their pool of excuses, which will land you nowhere.

Demand for a solution instead of complaints

Victims can be very irritating when they start talking about their never-ending complaints. To rectify this situation, ask the victim to come up with the solutions to their complaints. This will make them part of the solution instead of being victims.

Provide constructive feedback

As we have seen, victims have many excuses and will need you to respond to them. Victims want you to tell them that they did well and you understand why they did not accomplish their goals. You should be very careful when giving your feedback. You want to show them you understand what they are saying but do not legitimize their behavior or failures.

Compliment them

When dealing with an irritating victim, frequently give them compliments to encourage them to do more. For example, you can remind them of something they did well in the past, and then encourage them to carry on with that spirit. This positivity will rub off on them and it will eventually make them less irritating.

Help them prioritize their goals

You can diffuse the excuses of a victim by helping him or her put things into perspective. You can start by being honest about what needs doing. For example, you can say something like, "I hear what you are saying and I understand, but I need some results from you. How can I help you meet our expectations?"

The Rescuers Type

These types of people lose focus on what is important including their own productivity and responsibilities. The reason behind this is that they have convinced themselves that it is more important to take care of others than to complete their responsibilities.

Good examples of rescuers include the know-it-all, and the super agreeable types of difficult people. These types of people might appear helpful and hardworking at first, but in the end, you will come to learn they over-commit themselves and end up lugging behind in their responsibilities.

How to deal with rescuers

Explain the need to learn on their own

One way you can deal with a rescuer who is always bailing other people out is to explain why what they are doing is harmful to the development of others. For example, you can explain that if he or she keeps bailing the colleague, the said colleague might lose his or her job if he or she does not learn how to do it well. By helping out, they are doing more harm than good. Because of the desire to please, they will stop bailing the other person.

Be honest

The know-it-all in your organization may think he is the answer to every problem. You need to sit him or her down and be honest about how destructive overcommitment is to the organization. Explain to that person that he or she can serve the company better by excelling in his or her role rather than trying to be the savior in every department. Since their intention is to be the best, they will change for the good of the organization.

Limit spare time

The characters that these types of people possess are like an addiction to them. You can try to rehabilitate them all you want but if you do not get rid of their triggers, your efforts will be in futility. Their most pressing trigger is free time. This makes them want to go back to their bad behavior of rescuing others. Make sure you get rid of the spare time by assigning additional tasks and responsibilities.

Redirect their energy to a good cause

Dealing with a rescuer can be hard because they often do the wrong thing for the right reason. You can rectify this by redirecting their energy into something that will allow them to practice what they like in a positive manner. For instance, if you notice your employee is always helping everyone out and forgetting his/her job, you can promote them to be the new trainer of the department and give their responsibilities to someone else. That way, you will have a win-win situation.

Chapter 12: Find A Way To Communicate Or Work Together

Now that you have confronted the other person and let him/her know that you would like to find a way to communicate more effectively, it is time to find that way that will work for both of you. Although you have put forth a lot of effort here, going out of your way to be nice, say nice things, bring the topic to the table, your job is still not over.

After you have had that nice talk to Grandpa and reinforced how much you love him, offered to take him to the doctor and help him any way you can, you can also set up an agreement with him. If he is having a hard time, or feeling bad, or is in pain, he can call you and let you know and you will try to be there for him, or you will find someone who will be there for him. Set him up with a little book of names and phone numbers. For an elderly person who is alone, it is comforting to know that there is someone who cares, someplace that he can get some help. Then he will have no excuse for being grumpy or difficult.

When you have reached out to your neighbor and convinced him that you really want to be a good neighbor, and you offered him the opportunity to complain about noise, or anything else that may annoy him, he should then be ready to talk to you about it. Make a plan with him. Find out when his bedtime is and have your child practice his horn earlier in the day and not after a particular time at night—the same with music or television being too loud.

Now, with the coworker, you have had your little meeting; you have brought your feelings to his/her attention, and now you have asked all the right questions. He/she must now tell you how the two of you will continue to work together without emotional "warfare." If he/she is not ready or willing to work out a method that will work for both of you, then you have gone above and beyond to try to work things out with this person. At this point, you have 3 choices: (1) You can just deal with it, ignore the rudeness and avoid conversation with the person, (2) You can get a supervisor involved, or (3) you can ask to be transferred to a different department or look for another job. The last thing that you want to do is to feed into the rudeness by being rude back to the person. You may also come right out and tell the person that you will not tolerate his/her rudeness to you, and nicely ask him/her not to speak to you if there is nothing nice to say. You are doing your job and you will not allow him/her to interfere with you meeting your goals.

It is possible that standing your ground will get their attention, and they will turn their behavior around; but it is also possible that any attempts to solve this situation may be fruitless.

Chapter 13: Can You Be Friends With Your Employees?

Can you be friends with your employees? It's a tough call. I know a lot of managers who would scream "NO" to that one. I also know a lot of employees who wouldn't want to be friends with the boss anyway.

Being friends with employees certainly has a bad rap – and often, it has to be said, for perfectly legitimate reasons. It can be fraught with problems. Enjoying a friendship with a subordinate can leave you open to accusations of favouritism, the risk of being taken advantage of, or the danger of losing the respect of your other employees. Not to forget the fact that you may find it hard to manage these people in the way that you need to because they are your friends.

It's your job to be approachable but professional at all times; you need to gain and maintain your staff's respect. Bear in mind always that you will have to hold each and every one of your employees accountable at some point in the future; is that harder to do if they happen to be a good friend?

If you work with your friends, for instance, do you really want to 'boss' them around or tell them what to do? Do you shy away from actively managing them because you don't want to feel awkward when you're together over a beer or a glass of wine later? Are you more likely to ignore any shortcomings or problems with these people than any others, simply because you care for them and their feelings in a non-professional way? In short, because they are your friends and you want them to be happy, do you dread being the cause of any friction and try to avoid it at all costs? Do you worry that your friendship will suffer if your job gets in the way?

I know a lot of talented managers who prefer to keep their staff at arm's length for precisely that reason; they argue that it is impossible to "bollock" an employee if you've been out drinking with them. Do they have a point? Most certainly, yet some managers still seem to achieve it.

My personal experience is a case in point. I am currently still good friends with three of my former employees; granted that's just three people out of the many that I have managed in my career so far, so perhaps not such great odds. Still, it proves that it can happen.

So, what do these three lucky individuals have in common apart from the joy of my friendship? Funny you should ask. They do actually share one thing and it is probably the reason we were able to become friends in the first place: they were, for all intents and purposes, my seconds in command. They were the department heads, the section or team leaders; in short, they were my direct reports while their subordinates were one step removed from me. I had to trust these people to run the business the way I wanted it run; for the most part, I treated and thought of them as equals. They were also the only people I could share a moan with about the big boss.

Before you start to think that I'm the sort of manager who doesn't care about the "little people", let me be clear. I am the sort of manager who gets to know everyone who works for me; I don't believe in sitting in an office or being out of reach. And yet, I can't deny it; it's fair to say I'm not friends with anyone else, certainly no one further down the chain of management. I guess it either shows good taste on their behalf (joke!) or it proves what my manager cohorts have been telling me for years: you just can't be friends with your subordinates.

Of course, a great many managers choose to lead from a distance because they have been "burnt" in the past...

Sue's Story

"I had been working for the same company for 25 years, along with Mary, my best friend. Mary and I went on holiday together with our husbands, our children were close; we even lived just one mile from one another.

"When I was promoted to assistant manager, Mary was thrilled for me. At least that's how it started. Then the company hit trouble and we had no choice but to cut everyone's hours; that task fell to me. I worked out what I thought was a fair solution, sharing the pain around, but it didn't go down well. It became a mutiny; the staff began to make formal complaints and it became very bitchy, a lot of it aimed at me.

"Stupidly I thought Mary, as my best friend, would be the one person who would understand; true, the team were having a hard time but frankly so was I.

But she cut me dead; later I discovered she was the ring leader of the whole thing. What's more, she was the one making it personal. Even now, five years later, I still haven't forgiven her."

Look behind the protestations of those managers who insist that being friends with employees is an absolute no-no and you might well find that they have experienced something similar to Sue, whether on the same scale or smaller. It's human nature to want to be liked and appreciated; it's also human nature to put up walls to protect ourselves when we must.

The only downside to this, however, is that those managers who prefer to lead from a distance are missing a great motivational trick; you don't have to be friends with your team but you'll get much more out of them if you care about them and their welfare. You should strive for positive interpersonal relationships with your employees at all times.

According to Gallup, employees who have a close friendship with their manager are more than 2.5 times as likely to be satisfied with their jobs. Even if you don't want to be friends, those employees with a strong relationship with, or connection to, their managers are more likely to be loyal to the company (and work longer hours!). After all, we spend roughly 50% more time with our customers, colleagues and bosses than we do with the people we choose to spend time with - friends, partners, children and relatives - combined.

With that in mind, a Princeton University survey from the U.S. which asked participants to rate those people who they liked to spend time with, makes grim reading. At the bottom of a very long list was "the boss" – this was the person they least liked spending time with. In actual fact, interacting with the boss was rated "less enjoyable than cleaning the house". That's not a sentiment that you want your employees to share.

So, how do you "care" for your employees without crossing over into that friendship line, if that's how you choose to manage?

How to Show you Care

Well, among other things, you can:

Listen and empathise when they bring you problems but don't get emotionally involved and don't share your personal feelings with them.

Treat everyone fairly; favouritism never works.

If an employee shares a problem with you, offer them the tools they need to fix the problem but still hold them accountable for their results.

Be interested in your employees and take the time to greet them each day; in return, they will feel that they are valued in the company.

Take the time to join in team drinks and bonding sessions, but make sure you go out with everyone – not just a chosen few – and are not the last person standing (or not) at the end of the night.

Of course, in some cases you may already be working with your friends when you are promoted internally; can your friendship survive your new management role? Just as important, could your relationship actually derail your authority? If you're not careful, the answer could be yes, so here's a few tips on handling subordinates who started out as friends.

Don't finish your friendship the second you get promoted; that's a sure fire way to breed resentment.

Leave your friendship outside the workplace. Don't be chummy at work; such favouritism will breed resentment among your other workers.

Even when socialising outside the office, consider whether your behaviour will make it hard for your friend to respect you as his or her boss the morning after. (Beware the drunken bender!)

Set the ground rules up front and keep to them.

Don't talk shop when you're socialising; it's the easiest way to spill secrets you don't want to give away or to put your friend in an unfair position. Never share salary details, hiring and firing details or any other sensitive information you are privy to.

Don't ignore it if a friend is performing poorly at work; make sure you deal with it.

Likewise, be aware of any tendency to avoid conflict with your friend in particular. Is it because you don't want to damage your friendship? Make sure you treat your friend as fairly and equally as any other employee while in the workplace.

It's not an exaggeration to say that dealing with friendships at work can be a potential minefield. Even worse, there's no cut and dried guidelines to follow; it really is a personal decision. As the manager, you need to decide if it's in your nature to be friends with your employees, whether you can do so and still retain your professionalism and whether you want to.

The answer will depend on a myriad of different factors, including the personalities involved, the workplace culture and more.

I'm afraid that when it comes to the question – Can you be friends with your employees? – I have to admit that the answer is entirely up to you.

Chapter 14: An Incompetent Employee

An incompetent worker may well take a huge amount of your time; trying to guide, correct mistakes, respond to failures or generally deal with the fallout of an inept worker can take all a manager's energy, leaving precious little for the important things that really need to get done.

Who they are: It's important to recognise, of course, that making a few mistakes now and again doesn't make someone incompetent; if anything, it just makes them human. Instead an incompetent worker is someone who never seems to understand what they should be doing or how to do it. They are, quite frankly, useless to you.

Failing to deal with an employee who just isn't up to par not only breeds resentment from other staff who usually end up covering for the incapable worker but can actually chase customers away.

What to do: Once you have hired someone, you owe it to them to give them a chance to improve. So, talk to the employee about the problem; be honest and candid, try to find out what could be causing the incompetence and state clearly the standards that you expect from the employee. If the problem is significant, there's no getting away from the fact that you may very well have to hurt their feelings in order to have this conversation; no one likes to hear that they are not matching up. Just keep in mind that you are being cruel to be kind; you are raising the issue in order to give them the chance to improve before you have to take further disciplinary action.

That said, don't be afraid to discipline the employee if need be. Keep a close eye on the worker, giving them a steer every now and again as needed, or ask one of your tried and trusted employees to do it for you. You never know, the co-worker may be able to get through to the employee where you failed. Some people are so in awe of the boss title that they may be intimidated by you, rather than helped.

If things don't progress in the right direction, however, you should look at termination.

Staff who Bully the Boss

'Upward Bullying': When Staff Gang up on YOU!

Bullying is a common problem in Britain's workplaces; one in eight people have confessed to being bullied at work. The most common form of bullying is usually from the top down; no-one would deny that bully bosses have a lot to answer for. Co-workers can also make people's lives hell, but in recent years there has been another trend that not many people like to talk about – 'upward bullying'.

When a new manager comes on the scene, people like to test them. They will look for their weaknesses and test their patience; you could say we as adults haven't matured much past the need to play up for the substitute teacher in school. It's human nature to test out the boundaries and try to take advantage.

Who they are: Employees ganging up against the boss, most often a middle manager just like yourself, is finally being recognised as a problem. You may ask how subordinates could bully or harass a boss, but it's actually much easier to do than you probably realise. A determined bully or bullies can refuse to deliver messages, hide notes, fail to deliver important documents in time for a meeting, even give the manager the wrong version of the minutes... anything to make the manager look incompetent in front of other people and his or her direct boss. It's a highly effective strategy because it's very hard to prove; bosses are also unlikely to report it.

A survey by the Chartered Institute of People and Development found that 13 per cent of employees had been bullied at work in the six months before the survey; of those, 12 per cent admitted they had been bullied by a subordinate. In some cases of known bullying by subordinates, middle or line managers had been the victim of 'gang harassment' – a concerted effort by more than one member of the team to undermine them.

A bullying subordinate tends to be able to bully because they have a power over the manager in some way; it could be as simple as having the knowledge required to do a job or the information needed that a new manager does not have. If the manager is dependent upon that person or persons and the employee has a grievance, they can refuse to divulge that knowledge. As we have also heard, in some cases they can also deliberately try to orchestrate a plan to destabilise the manager.

The bullying can happen for a whole raft of reasons; it could be that the employee was passed over for your job before you arrived, or is close to someone who was. It could also be resentment that someone new has come in and wants to change things or it could be a case of shooting the messenger as you tackle some difficult changes to the team or company.

What to do: I said upward bullying is very hard to deal with and it's true. Even companies that have anti-bullying policies in place rarely have specific advice for the manager that is being bullied. Looking on the web won't help you either; there is a shocking lack of help available for a manager that finds him or herself in this situation.

The only way to treat the bullying, therefore, is as you would if you were a normal member of staff. No matter who is being bullied and at what level, it is the employer's responsibility to stamp it out. As such, you should speak to your immediate boss and HR to alert them to the problem.

Don't suffer in silence because you're embarrassed to admit what is going on; being a victim of bullying can lead to ill-health, problems with self-confidence and poor job performance – something you can't risk when you're the boss. You don't want to be forced out of your job so don't stand for it.

Before you go to HR or your boss to complain about the bullying, gather as much proof as you can. Document everything, no matter how small. Seek to prove your accusations. Seek support also from other managers; sometimes a fresh eye on events can be all that is needed.

In the meantime, take practical steps to reduce the opportunity for bullying; the bullying may directly impact on your ability to do your job so you need to protect yourself as much as you can. If you are reliant upon the bully or bullies for anything, for instance, try to arrange it so that the power they wield isn't quite so potent. If you don't need them anymore because you have learnt how to do their job, they have less solid ground to stand on.

Likewise, if they are messing around with your papers before you get in, for instance, lock them away in a drawer or your office. Take sensitive documents home with you; get someone you trust to send you the memos and take your calls. It may hopefully be that the bully gets bored when he or she can't cause mischief anymore.

Another common form of bullying is when staff try to dictate to the boss what should be done, or do whatever they want and not what the boss asks for. The fact is that you are in charge; don't let people tell you how you should behave or do your job. If they make suggestions and recommendations, by all means listen to them with an open mind but decide what you want to do in the end. If they argue with you, don't be afraid to say, 'I've listened to what you had to say and taken it into consideration, but I've decided we're going to do this instead', or 'I've heard your suggestions but as the manager I have to make the final choice and I want us to do this instead'.

Once you've issued your orders, don't back down. Chase up the work that you ask for and tackle it head on if they don't do it. Use disciplinary procedures if you have to and don't forget to keep copious notes on the instances you see. If you have a team of employees ganging up together, split them up. Either physically put them at different ends of the office, move one or more of them to different departments and/ or make a point of speaking to them about their behaviour one on one. People are much more likely to back down if they don't have their mates backing them up.

Start with an informal private meeting to see if you can resolve the problem. Be specific and polite but firm. Be careful if you decide to discipline the employee, however; it can often backfire on you if the employee makes a grievance report. That alone is one good reason why you should talk to HR or/ and your direct boss before taking any action; you need to protect yourself. If you are taken out of the equation, the employee can be disciplined without it falling back onto you.

Another good reason for informing your direct superior of what is going on is to take the wind out of the bully's sails. The bully or bullies want to make you look as if you can't do your job; if your boss knows about their tactics, he or she will know to ignore any apparent failings on your part until the problem is corrected. The bullies are probably also betting that you never will take the problem further and will suffer in silence; once they know that is not the case, they may feel it is too dangerous to continue with the behaviour.

An Employee with Substance Abuse Issues

This is a tricky problem; just how do you deal with an employee who you suspect has a drinking problem? Or someone who likes to roll in late after being out the night before with an obvious hangover? Is it just a bit of fun or could there be a serious addiction behind it?

Alcohol-related absenteeism is a real problem for UK businesses. Us Brits certainly like a drink, it's true, but surely it's going a touch too far when we lose between 8 and 14 million working days each year as a result. According to the

Health and Safety Executive, alcohol causes up to five per cent of all absences from work.

Absenteeism is just one consequence of alcohol. Others include poor productivity and performance, poor discipline, safety issues, a negative effect on morale as others must cover for the employee in question, lateness and, of course, the poor impression that it can give to customers.

And what if the problem goes deeper than the occasional blow out? What if you have an employee who seems to drink morning, noon and night, or an employee who is addicted to some other substance? Can you really work with such a person?

What to do: Employees with substance abuse issues can be difficult or nigh on impossible to manage; as well as low productivity and the potential safety hazard for themselves and others, they can be aggressive and, at times, even violent. They may also lie to the people around them and, if they are in thralls of chemical addiction, they may well resort to stealing.

As a manager, you and your employer have legal responsibilities when it comes to letting an intoxicated employee remain in the workplace. Under the Health and Safety at Work Act 1974, the company could be prosecuted if that employee then causes an injury to themselves or others.

So, if you suspect that an employee is imbibing during work hours, or that their out-of-hours drinking is impeding on their working life, what can you do?

First, you need to identify if there is a problem. This may well be obvious by the employee's behaviour, but otherwise you need to examine his or her sickness rates, productivity, accident records and any disciplinary reports. Putting them all together should give you enough information to assess if there is a problem or not.

If you think a particular employee has an alcohol problem, you need to appreciate that they are entitled to confidentiality and support, just as anyone with a medical condition or psychological problem would be. Try to consider it a health problem and not a disciplinary one, at least to begin with. It will be especially hard for someone to admit to having a drinking problem if they are worried about losing their job.

You should open the conversation by describing observable behaviours - what you or other members of the team have seen and observed about the employees behaviour - and state that you suspect they may be down to substance abuse.

You are within your rights to suggest they get expert help to deal with their alcohol problem but you cannot force them to do so.

You may feel sympathetic to them – they may be struggling with personal issues such as a marriage breakdown which has sent them off the rails – but never try to act as a counsellor for anyone with a mental health or addiction issue. Not only are you presumably not qualified to do so, but you may need to discipline them further down the line. That's hard to do if you're trying to counsel them at the same time.

Disciplinary action should, as always, be a last resort. If it does come to that, however, you must be able to show that you have exhausted all other possibilities before you terminate, otherwise you may find yourself at the end of an unfair dismissal case. You may well lose this if you cannot show that you tried to help the employee.

In order to tackle the wider problem of drinking during work hours or drinking that interferes with work, you may want to introduce an alcohol awareness policy, if your company does not already have one. This should set out exactly what is and isn't allowed in work time and inform all employees of any disciplinary action that may arise from it.

Let's take a look at how you, as a manager, could open discussion with an employee you suspect has a drinking problem, shall we?

Manager: Matthew, I want to talk to you about some behaviour that I and other people have noticed recently. Yesterday, you came in an hour late and took an extra hour for your lunch without informing anyone where you were. Later that afternoon you were found asleep in the break room. Two employees reported back to me independently that they smelt alcohol on your breath.

Last week, another employee raised the same concern after you were seen struggling to use your key card in the lock and I personally smelt alcohol on your breath at nine in the morning during our meeting last Wednesday.

I'm beginning to think you may have a drinking problem and, as your manager, I am concerned about you. I want to see what help I can offer you and see what we can do to tackle the impact of whatever is happening on your work and colleagues.

[Conversation continues...]

All of the previous employee situations can certainly test your patience and your management skills.

Finally, before we end this book, I want to say a quick word about another headache that novice managers and existing managers alike often struggle with and that is scheduling and dealing with a rota.

Conclusion

Difficult people are always around.

You have to learn how to deal with them effectively.

You must know how to identify them, know why they are so, and

how they can be dealt with.

Help them overcome their attitude.

The first thing to do before you can deal with difficult people is to

make sure that you are not a difficult person yourself. Otherwise, all efforts will be in vain.

Difficult people cannot help each other. They will rub against each

other and burn in the friction.

Someone mature and open-minded must enter their lives and

handle them without appearing obvious.

To be able to handle difficult people, you must have a good

character that is gentle, meek, patient, tolerant but firm in your

resolve never to become difficult yourself as you try to deal with

those who are. Then, you must know basic principles and techniques on how to deal with them, as laid out here.

It is useless to avoid dealing with difficult people. It will only

prove that you are no different from them, because difficult people avoid each other.

They never congregate.

Each difficult person wants to be the star. You cannot have all

difficult people in a group being the main attraction.

But they are everywhere; you cannot possibly avoid difficult

people all your life.

So the best option is to learn how to handle them properly.

When a problem remains unsolved, chances are, it will worsen or

multiply.

Difficult people left unattended will become your worst nightmare. We don't like them taking over the world. Thus, in a sense, dealing

with them is a calling. We have to help them to be able to help other people who are victimized by them.

And thus, we must also help ourselves.

And there's the likelihood of having difficult people in your family

- your spouse, children, sibling, or parents may be difficult people without you being aware of it.

You have to stop the difficulty from being widespread in your clan.

You have to face it and deal with it before things get out of hand.

Training your children is crucial in preventing difficult people from

emerging. It often starts in childhood.

Children left to themselves are potential candidates, especially

those whose every wish is fulfilled by doting adults, those who are

spared from proper discipline, and those who are abused and deprived from their parents' attention.

It is in childhood that a substantial molding takes place to produce mature individuals.

Finally, difficult people are people.

Don't hate or despise them. They are victims.

All of us have, in one time or another, been such victims. Their number one medicine is love.

Other supplements for their healing are understanding, patience,

and tolerance.

Your firmness in your maturity and uprightness will serve as their

eye openers.

You are the hope of difficult people near you. Don't fail them. They're counting on you.

www.ingramcontent.com/pod-product-compliance
Lightning Source LLC
Chambersburg PA
CBHW071451070526
44578CB00001B/305